CHANGE MINDSET PROGRAM

THE YOGIC WAY

A practical change management workbook connecting ancient sustainable leadership strategies with today's principles.

BY

GOMATHI SIVA SANKARAN

A GLAC – SADHANA INITIATIVE

The Guiding Light Art Company

Building bright futures through art and yoga

Made with ♥ on the Notion Press Platform

www.notionpress.com

Let's decode ancient wisdom together!

DEDICATION

SRI RAMA JAYAM

Gurur Brahmah Gurur Vishnuoh

Gurur Devo Maheshwarah

Guru Sakshaath Parah Brahmaah

Thasmai Sree Gurave Namah

Meaning – *Guru is the Brahma, the creator of knowledge, Guru is the Vishnu, the protector of wisdom, Guru is the Maheshwara, the destroyer of ignorance. Guru is the supreme almighty. Salutations to that revered Guru.*

This book is dedicated to my late grandfather, Retd. Prof. A. Sethu Pillai, my late grandmother, Mrs. Andal Sethu Pillai, my late mother Mrs. Meenakshi Sundari and my late father Mr. R. Siva Sankaran, the first four Gurus who brought me into this world and nurtured me with their wisdom.

This book is dedicated to all the Gurus that have guided me up to this point in my life either through their physical presence or through their knowledge sharing devices.

ACKNOWLEDGEMENTS

My sincere thanks to

- all the leaders and managers I have worked with during my stint with corporates. Many of them have been kind enough to mentor me and let me find my goal and its purpose.
- Kirsten Andersen, my first mentor in Denmark. Every time, I felt stuck, her magical 2x2 matrices helped me find a new way.
- Professor John Hayes, for his inspiring lectures on Change Management at the Copenhagen Business School's Full-Time MBA Program.
- all the families and friends that saw me through my personal losses and challenges.
- everyone that has been a part of the creation of the Guiding Light Art Company or GLAC's startup journey.
- Srividhya Mothilal for the cover page design.
- Tobias Lasota for seeing the value in my script and supporting me in turning the same into visual content, which is now taking shape in this book. Thanks for co-creating the GLAC Sadhana
- the proofreaders Manoj Kumar Karthikeyan and Nina Rose Simonsen for having reviewed the entire content in about 10 days and helped in bringing its best version out into this world.

Contents

DEDICATION 5

ACKNOWLEDGEMENTS 7

Foreword 11

Chapter 1: UNDERSTANDING OUR OWN MINDSET 13

Chapter 2: STRATEGIES FOR DEVELOPING A GROWTH MINDSET – GOAL Vs. PURPOSE 17

Chapter 3: THE GROWTH MINDSET SHOWSTOPPER – ANGER MANAGEMENT 22

Chapter 4: IMPORTANCE OF VISION IN GROWTH MINDSET & UNDERSTANDING STAKEHOLDERS 28

Chapter 5: OUR MINDSET AND WELLBEING 33

Chapter 6: GROWTH MINDSET - BIAS Vs. GOAL 37

Chapter 7: CRISIS MANAGEMENT 42

Chapter 8: CONFLICT MANAGEMENT & DECISION MAKING 48

Chapter 9: COMMUNICATION & RELATIONSHIP MANAGEMENT 54

Chapter 10: SUSTAINABLE RESOURCE MANAGEMENT 62

CONCLUSION 67

Bibliography 71

Glossary 73

About the Author 76

Foreword

Thank you for choosing to read this book.

Owing to my work exposure, travelling, studying, and living in countries other than that of my origin, I am accustomed to certain globally renowned change leadership principles and practices. I have had the privilege to be a part of some success stories. On the other hand, I have painfully watched interesting projects close abruptly, amazing teams crumble down, and dreams shatter.

If today's leadership principles and practices are highly efficient, then why are we facing situations such as war, global warming, and scarcity of resources?

Be it organizations or individuals, we all mean well when we kick-start any idea. Where do we go wrong in the process of turning that idea into a goal? So much so, that we rely on unsustainable means to get there?

For many years, I trusted in the process that was given to me everywhere I worked or travelled. What if there's something fundamentally wrong with these processes? Or maybe we have missed out certain parts of the equation causing this global imbalance. Which part of this process needs a change?

That's when I turned to history. I turned to those lessons and stories I had learned when I was a child. It amazed me to learn for the second time in my life as a grown up, that there existed dynasties that had ruled large topographies for hundreds and thousands of years. Sustainable leadership?!?! How?!? I wondered.

This is where my quest for a glorious and sustainable world started. I am still in the process of decoding such stories. Thankfully, I am not the only one doing this! So far, I have understood that today's processes or approaches aren't entirely wrong. They aren't entirely sustainable either. There are some missing pieces in this global puzzle we all are playing.

This book is my first attempt to share these missing pieces in a light and friendly format. This book attempts to help you to switch the gear – building the growth mindset in a sustainable way – the yogic way.

- The 10 chapters in this book will take you through some of the known leadership and change concepts through the lens of our forefathers.
- Each chapter will start with a short story from the past.
- There will be pauses in-between the story for you to reflect and become a part of this book. Yes! You get to complete my book.
- There will also be some action points for you to take away or to try putting into practice.

This book does not intend to give you a one-size-fits-all solution. My purpose for writing this book is to share with you some perspectives that could possibly be added to your pre-existing worldview. These slight changes to your approach could in turn add value to your journey towards success.

I will introduce you to the Guru Parampara of learning and knowledge sharing. The good-old method of breaking down hard-hitting concepts into simple thought processes and sugar-coating the same with stories.

Hope you enjoy this learning and knowledge sharing experience!

Chapter 1

UNDERSTANDING OUR OWN MINDSET

The first ever step to understanding change is to start from within. There can be elements both internal and external that induce change. However, the most important element in change is 'YOU' – what is your response to change? What is your relationship with change?

Here comes a small story that will help you gauge your own mindset and its relationship with change.

The Story:

Get ready to travel back in time!

Our little time machine inside our brain is going to take us back to about 1000 years in history. We have just arrived in a tiny village somewhere in the central part of India. Nearby the village under the shades of a large tree sits a Guru meditating and contemplating. The lifestyle of the Guru or the teacher in those days, was way different than we can imagine today.

Most of the Gurus preferred to and were also expected to lead the life of simplicity. That involved having almost nothing in the name of 'possession'. All a Guru possessed were the clothes on his back and an empty bowl. In the afternoons he roamed around the village asking for alms – "Bhavathi Bikshaam dehi!" meaning "the lady of the house please offer something" to eat. The act of being as humble as possible, that when it comes to offering knowledge, the Guru can freely do so without any egoistic thoughts, is the core idea behind this lifestyle. Whether somebody offers him something or not isn't a matter of concern to the Guru. He is always content with whatever comes his way.

One fine day, this Guru takes his afternoon walk around the village and randomly enters this household wherein the man of the house doesn't have a proper job yet, has a wife and three kids to feed. If he gets lucky then he does some errands for others and earns wages, which was his Plan A. As one can predict easily, luck doesn't favour this man much. Hence, he and his family mostly rely on their Plan B in life – a Ghewada creeper that grows in their front yard. A ghewada creeper is typically a kind of spinach, which the man's wife plucks out every day and makes a soup out of. That's essentially the diet for the whole family!

This very fine day when the Guru enters this house and asks "Bhavathi bikshaam dehi!" the woman goes out to her yard, plucks a few leaves from the creeper, makes the soup, and offers the same to him.

The entire 'hungry' family watches as the Guru finishes his sumptuous meal. Once done, the Guru gets up to leave and blesses the whole family to have a 'prosperous life'.

On his way out the Guru sees the ghewada creeper. He goes close to the creeper, snatches it off and breaks it into pieces and walks out without turning back!

Let's pause the story here!

Reflection time:

Let's just take a moment to reflect on the mindset of the poor man and his wife. Most importantly their hungry children

Let's also reflect on why the Guru chose to do what he just did?

What is your mindset with respect to this situation? Especially when you place yourself in the shoes of this family.

Take a moment to write down your thoughts here:

Action Point:

The first step to understanding your mindset is to first start observing your own breath. While reading this story and reflecting on the situation, how were you breathing?

When given some fresh inputs your brain starts processing. At any point in time, the brain needs to have certain levels of fresh circulatory air to function effectively. Just a fresh breath of air could help you make a switch in your mindset.

On average, a human brain typically needs ½ litre of tidal volume + 2 litres of inspiratory volume +1 and ½ litres of expiratory volume (i.e.) approximately 4 litres of air circulation to be at its best.

Now, could you try to sit comfortably and take a deep breath in and out a couple of times via your nostrils?

By just doing this you are helping your brain to have the time and space to process the information better. Of course, this change doesn't happen within just a couple of breaths. Throughout this book as and when you hit a 'reflection area' or an 'action point' just try reminding yourself of that and let's see the impact as the pages progress. Slowly try incorporating this deep breath mechanism each time you are faced with complex problem solving or decision making.

Back to the story…

Yes, you guessed it right! There is chaos and conflict in the family. With the children crying out of hunger, and the lady shouting in despair at her husband – the scenario is nothing less than depressive. The poor man is feeling defeated and helpless. He watches everything that is happening around him in despair. However, he muscles up the courage to have a look around at what is left of the plant and what can possibly be done to control the damage.

He sees the broken branches of the creeper and notices that the Guru had pulled the creeper out, but not its roots. He sees a possibility that the roots could be removed from the soil and replanted in another spot in his yard and maybe one day, it will start putting up fresh branches and leaves. He tries his best to console his wife and children saying that the Guru might have some higher reason for such a deed. Due to the absence of food for now, we can't clearly understand the Guru's intention. The family isn't convinced though.

He still sets out to do whatever he could. He gets a crowbar and carefully pulls out the roots from the earth. Looks around for a better spot wherein the creeper would get good sunshine, be well protected, and starts digging a new trench into the earth for his creeper's roots to go in to.

Reflection Time:

Let's compare the mindsets of the poor man and his wife with your notes on the previous reflection exercise. Now that we have a tool to ensure that our brain works effectively for us, let's share our thoughts here with the fresh breath of air:

Back to the story…

Developing a growth mindset stems from the understanding of losses and using them as a stepping stone to find an alternative. Though the poor man was equally depressed about the situation, he began reviewing the losses and contemplating the alternatives.

He began digging further when he felt something stopping him. When the crowbar hit powerfully down on the earth, he could feel a strong resistance. He pulls it back with full force and uses all his power to send it back deeper into the earth – "DUNG!!!!!"

The metal hit something hard which was stopping it from moving further down.

He tried one more time, with full energy – he raises the crowbar up and pushes it down on the earth – "DUNG!!!"

This sound is so loud and hard, as though metal is crushing onto another metal. There must be something inside stopping it!

He is now curious. He throws away the crowbar and starts using his arms and legs to sense what is stopping him. Slowly and steadily the metal that was stopping him presents itself. Only what he finds is not just a piece of metal – it is a large pot filled with GOLD COINS!

The 3-part perspective to growth mindset:

All through his tragic life, this gold-filled pot was lying right under his nose! For him to realize this, there were 3 key action points needed:

- The guru pulled the ghewada creeper out, pushing him out of the comfort zone.
- The poor man began thinking out of the box by pulling the creeper's roots from the earth and trying to find another place for it.
- While doing so, the poor man had exercised "a detached attachment" towards the situation. In a way, he had emotionally disconnected himself from the state that he saw his whole family was in.

Action Points:

To build on our growth mindset we will have to approach our challenges in this 3-part perspective:

- Leave comfort zone.
- Think out of the box.
- Practice detached attachment.

Chapter 2

STRATEGIES FOR DEVELOPING A GROWTH MINDSET

GOAL Vs. PURPOSE

Now that we have learnt a little more about our own mindset and how we can use some simple tools to practice switching our mindset towards a growth path, let's delve a little deeper into goal setting. On agreeing that we have decided to grow our mindset, we need to decide where to? Where do you want to go? How far? And most importantly why?

The Story:

Let's launch ourselves into this time machine that is taking us back about 1000 years.

We are again in the precincts of a village waiting for our Guru. Oh! By the way, he doesn't stay in or near one village for long. He practices detached attachment, so he prefers travelling around and not really sticking to or building his own comfort zone.

This time around, our Guru is walking in a deep dark forest. He has a stag or stick in his hand to help him traverse through the forest terrain. He is barefooted and can therefore sense the slush muddy range that he is walking through. Suddenly, he feels something hard tugging at his feet from below. He kneels carefully down and uses his finger to poke into this unknown element that has halted his journey. He finds a piece of jewellery. Not just any jewellery – this happens to be unique in a way that it holds precious gems on it. One can make a fortune out of this single piece!

Let's take a pause here.

Reflection Time:

What do you think the mindset of the Guru will be? What will be your mindset if you were the one finding such a precious jewel?

Back to the story…

The Guru chuckles at his new finding, slips it into the small cloth pouch hanging around his hip and walks along until he reaches the next village. After having found a nice shady tree, the Guru settles down and looks around. Curious villagers approach the Guru to get acquainted with him when he opens his pouch and shows them the glittery piece of jewellery.

He tells them, "Since I'm a renunciate it doesn't make sense to have this jewellery as my possession. Hence, I have decided to hand this over to the poorest and most needy person that I meet."

No sooner than the Guru makes such an announcement, the villagers start lining up in front of him, pouring out their personal, financial, mental, physical, and emotional challenges. Each one is eagerly awaiting the Guru to declare him/her as the 'poorest and most needy' and hand over this precious piece. The Guru, on the other hand, listens, listens, and listens to all their grievances with full attention patiently. He even asks the 'why-question' as many times as possible, to dig deeper into their needs and their ultimate purpose. His eyes show the compassion he has for every single story. However, he doesn't seem to have the intent to give away the jewellery to anyone!

The news spreads like wildfire, reaching a few more villages. Therefore, people start travelling from far and wide to meet this Guru who could potentially change their lives. The stories range from personal tragedies to grave health issues, to business needs. There were also people who wanted money for building roads, schools, hospitals, temples, and such, so they could not only help themselves but also help a community in the process.

Still no sign of our Guru deciding on who should be the receiver.

Let's take a pause here.

Reflection Time:

What will be the mindset of the people? What is the mindset of the Guru? What is your mindset at this moment?

Action Point:

Imagine you were to make an elevator pitch of your goal to this Guru (like what every villager is doing). Write down your ultimate goal and use the 5-whys principle to further elaborate on the same.

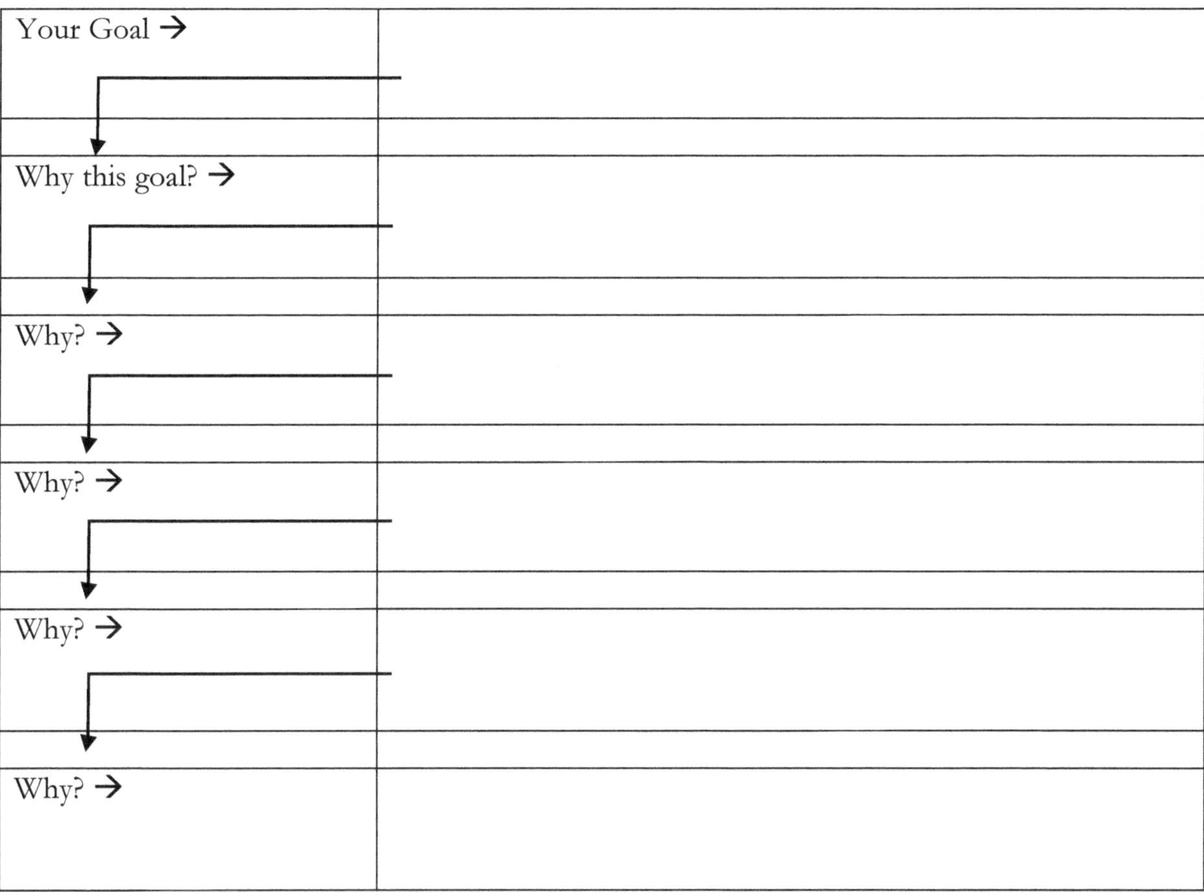

Your Goal →	
Why this goal? →	
Why? →	
Why? →	
Why? →	
Why? →	

Back to the story…

As days pass by, the story of the Guru with the precious piece of jewellery reaches different cities and people start travelling long distances in hope to get this piece. The word reaches the King of the country. The King is a very busy man. He is passionate about war and acquiring more terrain to expand his kingdom. So, he is seldom in the country. The moment he wins a war and acquires another country, he starts planning his next move. He will not stop until he becomes the emperor of the whole world.

He doesn't appreciate this idea of an unknown Guru from a remote corner of his country being discussed so widely and getting all the attention. So, he initially sends his ministers and guards to check out. They come back and report to him that the Guru seems to be genuine. However, it is not possible for them to decipher as to why he hasn't given up on this possession yet. They even explained some of the sample situations that they had heard from the villagers and who they felt, deserved to have received it.

The daily report on this situation disturbs the King so much that he finally decides to make his personal visit to the spot. When he arrives at this humble place that is now overcrowded with people, he is astonished to see that so many people need something to move on with their lives. He also watches the people discuss their problems with the Guru and is heavily annoyed at the Guru's inability to decide.

The King now walks up to the Guru and says "oh! Guru! What sort of a commotion have you created in my country? Are you not able to decide who deserves this jewellery or are you trying to play them as fools?"

The Guru smiles and says nothing.

Agitated, the King speaks in a harsh tone, "Do you even know who I am!? Do you have any idea of the wealth I possess!! This piece of jewellery might be important to you and those assembled here. Yet it is a sheer piece of stone in my hands!"

Saying this, the King thrusts his hand in front of the Guru. In the same moment, the Guru places this jewellery in the hands of the King!

Let's take a pause here.

Reflection Time:

What is the mindset of the King – the ultimate receiver of this jewellery?

What will be the mindset of the people? What is the mindset of the Guru?

What is your mindset at this moment?

Action Point:

Let's discuss the term 'GOAL' in the light of leadership. Both the King and the Guru are leaders in their own manner. Do you think their individual goals have a purpose? Being the leader of your own goal, can you define the purpose of your goal?

Back to the story…

Well, the new owner of the jewellery is not a happy man! The King feels heavily insulted in front of his own people when the Guru handed it over to him and in a way declared him to be the "poorest and most needy person".

The King is lost for words and looks at the Guru questioningly.

Evidently, he needs some help in understanding why he was the chosen one.

So, the Guru says, "Oh, my King! A SRIMAN is a person that is abundantly wealthy. There are three signs to identify such an abundantly wealthy person:

- One who has a goal with a purpose.
- One who is selfless.
- One who is making a steady progress."

"When I heard the tragic stories of your people, understood their needs, and further asked them to explain their goals, I could clearly see that they all had purpose. Most of them were selfless and were making steady progress to reach their goals despite all the challenges. They will continue to do so even without this piece of jewellery."

The Guru elaborated further, "Your people have grief. They also have the courage to fight their grief. When grief meets courage, the constructive efforts arise. Today their financial status might be "poor". However, this status does not determine who they are! Their goals with clear and concise purpose, their acts of selflessness, and their ability to make progress renders them to be SRIMAN".

"You! Oh King! Seem to have set yourself up for a goal to rule the world when most of your people are in grave need for support and encouragement! Where is the purpose in your goal?"

"If an unknown Guru from the remote corner of your country is able to get the status of how most of the people in this country are feeling, just by sitting under a tree with a piece of jewellery, my dear King, you have the power to leverage your resources effectively and ensure that your kingdom and its people are taken care of adequately!"

The King realises his lapse and thanks the Guru for this lesson.

Action Point:

Let's put your goals and purpose to the SRIMAN test:

- Do you have a goal with a clear and concise purpose?
- Is the goal and purpose selfless?
- Are you making steady progress however slow it might be?

Chapter 3

THE GROWTH MINDSET SHOWSTOPPER

ANGER MANAGEMENT

Isn't it fantastic that we know our mindset and have our goals chalked out with clear and concise purpose! Aren't we wealthy! Guessing whether the next typical step is probably a SWOT analysis? Well, the yogis and Gurus differed slightly from our current day approach. They saw anger as a huge showstopper to the growth mindset. Let's see why.

The Story:

Our time machine is taking us to meet a slightly angry Guru this time. Fasten your seatbelts. Let's go back in time!

We are in the precincts of a sleepy village, where a couple have just given birth to a child. This child seems unusually bright in his appearance – there's a sort of radiance about him that attracts people to him from the day he was born. Everyone that meets him says that he's probably destined to do something great in life. The proud parents name him Kaushika and they do their best to provide him with whatever he had wanted.

The developing years of Kaushika were filled with books, scriptures, and activities. He didn't only want to gain knowledge but also achieve excellence. At a tender age, Kaushika decides to become a sage and seek wisdom. He decides to leave his parents in search of wisdom. His parents, on the other hand, wish to have him with them all the time and hope that he will take care of them when they get old. The heartbroken parents had to let him go because they knew that this village was too small for his goals.

Kaushika, now a renowned, well-travelled Guru who has so much success and accolades, is wandering across the nation with a feeling of emptiness. He feels that he is missing the divine joy and decides to meditate rigorously. After wandering for few days, he reaches the precincts of a village and finds a Peepal tree to sit under and meditate with single-minded focus.

It is evening time now. Kaushika has lost the understanding of time though, now that he's been seated for a while meditating. The evening time around these supposedly quiet villages filled with trees, is not really calm. It is the time for birds to get back to their nests. One can hear the chirping of the birds. On this fine evening, a crow and a crane end up on the very same peepal tree and for some reason decide to have a fight.

Kaushika is irritated by these sounds and tries his best to 'shoo' them away. Some of the birds fly away. However, the crow and crane are fully engaged in their fight oblivious of the highly disturbed Guru. It is unacceptable that such tiny birds could derail our Guru from his goals. Kaushika's temper and voice raises. Yet, the fight goes on.

Kaushika's anger reaches a level where his third eye in between his eyebrows open and there comes a lava of fire that lashes out at these two birds. Within a second, a dead crow and crane fall from the peepal tree. Complete silence.

Let's take a pause here.

Reflection Time:

What are your thoughts on Kaushika's goals and his anger?

What are your goals in life? Are there any crows and cranes derailing you from your goals?

Action Point:

After your reflection, could you further elaborate on those crows and cranes that are disturbing you?

Are they internal or external? Also guesstimate the level of anger you feel in them as a percentage and the time you will need to recover.

Type (internal/external) of crow/crane	Your anger level in percentage	Time needed for your mind to recover

Back to the story…

Well, the angry Guru Kaushika tries to meditate. However, this unusual stillness caused by his action disturbs him. He's also hungry. So, he decides to take a break and walk into this new village trying to find food. He randomly chooses a house, walks in, and says "Bhavathi bikshaam dhehi". The lady of the house comes out and says, "you are welcome, dear sir!" and adds, "I am just about to prepare food. If you can please come into the house, take a seat in the portico, I will proceed with the cooking and bring the food when ready".

Kaushika now settles down while watching what this woman is doing. There are two elderly people in the house who seem to be incapacitated. So, the woman is going around taking care of them, cleaning them and such. She's also going about with her cooking simultaneously. However, all her actions put together takes a lot of time. One thing unique about her demeanour is that she's doing each task with full devotion, contentedness, and tranquil. There is a kind of unusual peacefulness in stark contrast to the visuals unfolding in front of Kaushika's eyes. Our angry and hungry Guru gets more irritated though. Finally, when the cooking is done the woman goes about feeding the elderly people first and offers the remaining food to Kaushika.

This action aggravates Kaushika's anger, and he roars at the woman, "Lady! Do you even know who I am and how precious my time is? You have taken so much time to prepare the food! I'm so angry!!! Do you know the powers that I possess and what the consequences of your actions will be?"

The lady in her calm and balanced voice replies, "My dear sir! I am neither a crow nor a crane to get burned down by your anger."

Stunned at this response, Kaushika wonders how this household woman deciphered the peepal tree incident.

The lady continues, "It was never my intention to delay or insult you in any way. I am just a simple householder that is going about her responsibilities. As the lady of the house, I am responsible for the health and welfare of my father-in-law and mother-in-law. You can see that both are old and incapacitated. So, they need my help and care. All I know of, is to perform my duties with full attention and care. My apologies to you if my actions have disturbed you in any way. Please eat the food."

Surprised Kaushika now responds, "no, no, my lady! You need not apologize. I am a Guru in search of the divine joy or bliss, which I find so present in you. I want to learn from you how you have attained the same. Will you be so kind as to teach me?"

The lady answers, "Dear sir, with all my current responsibilities, I unfortunately do not see how I can be of any help to you. However, I can suggest someone who can best show you the way to supreme bliss. His name is Dharmavyadha, and he lives in the city of Mithila."

"Thanks for your kindness and help, my dear lady! I bless you and your family with good health and happiness. I will now take leave." Says Kaushika and starts on his new journey towards the city of Mithila.

He is now happy that he not only found delicious food but also a direction for his goal. There's someone who can help him achieve his goal. He must be a Guru for all the Gurus! Must be someone with special powers! His imagination runs faster than his feet. When he reaches the city of Mithila, he asks around for Dharmavyadha and the people guide him with the route. He finally reaches the street where he is to meet his ultimate Guru. As he proceeds to walk, he notices that the street is covered in blood and the smell of the street is appalling! He's now totally confused. He double-checks with the people around who confirm that it is the street where Dharmavyadha lives. He walks into the butcher-street of Mithila city.

Let's take a pause here.

Reflection Time:

Let's reflect on Kaushika's mindset.

Could you reflect on any situation(s) wherein your ego/anger/frustration has played against you?

Action Point:

Further elaborating on your reflection can we find some patterns? Please use this table to list the situations wherein your emotions, especially anger, has derailed you from your goals or has helped you with your goals.

Describe the situation	ANGER - FOR or AGAINST your goal?

Back to the story…

Kaushika, a pure vegetarian all his life, is perturbed by the incidents that have happened in the past few hours. He had killed two birds and is now taking a walk on the butcher street to meet an unknown person.

Dharmavyadha (the divine butcher) sees the confused Kaushika and waves at him, "welcome sir! you must be the Guru that the lady had sent from the village".

Before Kaushika could respond, he further adds with a smile, "this is my shop, sir. Please be seated here while I finish with my customers. Then I will take you to my home that is behind the shop."

Kaushika tries to find a clean and dry spot in this messy butcher's shop and settles down.

Dharmavyadha goes about slashing animals and birds, peeling their skins off, cutting the meat into pieces, while he is engaging in conversation with his customers. Kaushika's stomach is ready to push everything it has out of his mouth. He holds a towel tight to his nostrils and mouth, trying his best to hold back from puking. In about 5 to 10 minutes, when his body and mind get acclimated to the scenario, Kaushika starts observing his host's actions with full attention.

Overpowering the voices of judgement, Kaushika notices the peacefulness in Dharmavyadha's smile and actions. It is a butcher's house. Yet, there is divine joy in this place. The personal attention that Dharmavyadha gives to each customer, makes the customer also feel the peace. He is in fact spreading peace and joy in his actions. How is this possible? He's killing animals for a living after all!

Having had a bit of training on patience at the lady's house, Kaushika decides to wait for his host to be done with his job. When Dharmavyadha is fully done attending to all his customers, he closes his shop and takes the awaiting Guru inside his residence. The humble home also hosts two incapacitated old people – Dharmavyadha's parents.

Kaushika realizes that Dharmavyadha's day has just begun. As anticipated, Dharmavyadha carries his old parents like as though they are his children, gives them a bath, puts fresh clothing on them, and makes them rest, while he starts cooking. Once the cooking is done, he feeds his parents first and then brings the remaining food to serve Kaushika. All actions done with full attention and care – divine joy in the making!

Kaushika tries to start the conversation politely choosing the words, "you see Dharmavyadha, I appreciate the efforts that you take and the blissful emotions that you bring not just to yourself, but also to every person that you meet. However, I think in your best interest that you should reconsider your career."

Dharmavyadha smiles and replies, "my dear sir, the present job that I have is my karma – my duty. I have accepted all my duties towards the people of the city and towards my family wholeheartedly. Neither do I judge, nor do I compare between my actions and the actions of others. When one has submitted oneself wholeheartedly to every moment of every action one easily attains divine bliss."

"You seek the divine joy, my dear sir", said Dharmavyadha, "you are well-versed in scriptures and such, and this you have achieved through your SADHANA (practice). For one to excel in anything Sadhana, much is required of you. However, Sadhana is not just ABHYAS (doing the things that ought to be done). Even VAIRAGYA (refraining from doing the things that ought not to be done), is an integral part of Sadhana."

Kaushika begins understanding what was missing in his Sadhana.

Dharmavyadha continues, "Anger is the single greatest enemy that dwells in the heart of a human, dear sir. Once you set your Vairagya on anger, your Sadhana is bound to fructify."

Kaushika thanks Dharmavyadha for his hospitality. He's now clear about his next destination. It is his parents' village, where Kaushika resumes living his life more meaningfully together with his parents, serving them and sharing his knowledge with the people around.

Action Point:

Now that we know how much time and energy we have spilt on our anger from our previous exercise, let's use this easy formula to practice achieving our goals.

ABHYAS + VAIRAGYA = SADHANA

List the core activities you must get done to achieve your goals in the following format:

Activity Nr.	SADHANA (Practice)	ABHYAS (ought to be done)	VAIRAGYA (ought not to be done)
Activity 1			
Activity 2			
Activity 3			

Chapter 4

IMPORTANCE OF VISION IN GROWTH MINDSET & UNDERSTANDING STAKEHOLDERS

We have refined our mindset and goals in the past chapters. Most importantly, we have a newfound formula for practice, so our mindset is fully aligned with our goals. Now it is time to put these goals through the vision test. Let's jump right in!

The Story:

Let the time machine take us back to another Guru.

Our Guru this time is someone who loves taking long walks. Every morning and evening, he takes a stroll alongside the village pastures to reach a riverbank where he takes his bath. There are also farmlands along the way that he walks. One of the farmers is a devotee of the Guru and looks forward to the time when the Guru takes his walk close to his farmland. Every time he sees the Guru, he bows down, falls at the feet of the Guru, and takes his blessings.

As days pass by, the Guru takes note of this consistency in the farmer's approach and decides to have a short conversation with him. He asks the farmer why he looks forward to his blessings every day. The farmer replies that he feels positivity each time he sees the Guru and thinks that this is the reason for his success in life. The Guru smiles at him and asks, "What do you want from me?"

"Dear Guru", the farmer replies, "all I would ever want from you would be your blessings and nothing more".

The Guru smiles and enquires as to what the farmer does. The farmer requests the Guru to come over to his farmland and shows him the jowar crop that he cultivates on his land.

"You have a nice farmland here. Do you own it?" asks the Guru.

"No, my Guru. I pay the owner of this farmland a certain amount of the crop yields every year" says the farmer. "With your blessings, I have always been successful in my jowar crop farming. Never had a single crop failure."

The jowar crop had put in tender ears and it looked like the crops will be ready to harvest in about a month.

"Do you trust me?" asks the Guru.

"Yes, of course my Guru!" exclaims the flustered farmer.

"Then, I think, you must chop off your crop today". Says the Guru and walks off to the riverbank for his daily bath.

Let's take a pause here.

Reflection Time:

What is the mindset of the farmer?

What is the mindset of the Guru?

What would be your response if it were your crops?

Action Point:

List the moments in your life when you had almost reached your goal, however, were stopped by something or someone. How have your reacted in such situations and why?

1

2

3

Back to the story…

The farmer doesn't know the intentions behind the Guru's words however trusts in him unconditionally. Therefore, he decides to follow the instructions. However, he is fully aware of the consequences of his actions. There are stakeholders that will be affected by his actions.

The farmer rushes home immediately, takes out a portion of the crop yield from last year from his barn, to pay off his landlord. Sets aside some of the yield for his family and to pay off his workers.

He informs his family that they will have to survive on last year's remaining yield for a whole year. He informs the landlord of his decision to chop off the crop and asks him to accept this year's payment in advance. He then gets his team to chop off the jowar crop.

His actions create a lot of commotion in the village. The landlord, his family members, his workers and even the farmers from the neighbouring lands question his decision. He explains that it is his Guru's will, and he will act on it at once.

"You are totally out of your mind!" exclaims the landlord "You have always paid your dues on time. You are trying to pay off in advance, which I can accept, and I will not interfere in your decision. However, this decision is foolish!"

"What if we do not make any yield in the coming year and we run out of stock?" asks the wife, "How do you propose that we feed our family?"

"It is your business though. We are only neighbours" commented the other farmers "Yet, what do you think a sage will know about farming? Why should you listen to his words?"

"You are our master, and we will follow your directions" said the workers, "We are worried for our future though."

The farmer had made up his mind and nothing can stop him now. So, the workers proceed to chop the crops off.

The Guru, on his way to the riverbank for his evening bath, notices the drastic change in the farmer's land. "What have you done?" asks the Guru.

"You had wanted the crops to be chopped off, my Guru" replies the farmer.

"Oh! But I had just mentioned that jokingly", responds the Guru, "I never thought one will take my joke so seriously."

"Your wish is my command, my Guru", says the farmer, "I trust in you and your words. Hence, I do not regret this decision even if it was an outcome of a joke".

Let's take a pause here.

Reflection Time:

Share your thoughts on this situation.

Action Point:

Showstoppers vs. stakeholders.

Elaborate on the situations from your previous exercise. How many stakeholders did you have? How was your interaction with each stakeholder? Also categorize these stakeholders into those who are (1) an integral part of your goal (i.e.) you are expected to involve them in your decision-making, (2) not directly involved in your decision-making however have any influence on your decisions, and (3) neither directly involved nor influential.

Showstopper situations	Stakeholders	Stakeholder Category	Your interaction/actions

Back to the story…

Within a week of this incident, the entire area is hit by a heavy cyclone that ravages farmlands and houses and leaves its people with nothing to hold onto. On our farmer's land though, only the stacks had remained due to his decision to chop off the tender corns. The stacks survived the storm and now that they have been watered adequately, very slowly they start putting fresh stalks. Due to the chopping off process, the stacks even branch out thereby multiplying the tender corn growth. In a couple of months, the farmer ends up producing a triple yield as compared to that of his previous years. He employs more people and tries to support the neighbouring farmers that have faced huge losses.

The VISION – Big Picture

The farmer had principally followed all the known methods of production similar to that of his neighbours, which did give him success in the previous years. The Guru challenged him in a way, that he can do two things:

- Be prepared to face exceptional situations.
- Learn to handle all the stakeholders.

Though the farmer took the decision to cut his crops out of his devotion and respect for his Guru's words, he didn't stop himself from reaching out to all his stakeholders. He was polite with them all. However, he chose to compensate some of his stakeholders who will directly be affected by his actions. He made crop reserves for some of his stakeholders. At the same time, he chose to ignore the comments of people who were neither directly involved nor influenced his decision.

The key to stakeholder management is to identify each of stakeholders at an early stage of your goal and to know when and how to involve them in your actions. When this strategy is combined with a big picture understanding of our goal, will further strengthen your goal.

Action Point:

Now let's build our combo pack of SWOT and Stakeholder analysis. In every aspect of our business or individual goal, there's a stakeholder involved. What is your SWOT and who are your stakeholders? How much of an involvement and/or influence do they have in your SWOT?

STRENGTHS (External elements affecting your goal)			
Strength	**Stakeholder(s)**	**Involvement %**	**Influence %**
WEAKNESSES (External elements affecting your goal)			
Weakness	**Stakeholder(s)**	**Involvement %**	**Influence %**
OPPORTUNITIES (Internal elements affecting your goal)			
Opportunity	**Stakeholder(s)**	**Involvement %**	**Influence %**
THREATS (Internal elements affecting your goal)			
Threat	**Stakeholder(s)**	**Involvement %**	**Influence %**

Chapter 5

OUR MINDSET AND WELLBEING

We are growing our idea into a business plan, while we ensure that our mindset grows along and strengthens. Our goal has a purpose, vision, and an understanding of its stakeholders. Now it is time to ensure that you, as an individual, are fit as a fiddle to lead this idea towards success.

The Story:

Our time machine is taking us to Kalingadesam. The period is approximately between 1100 and 261 BCE. Kalingadesam is about 70% of today's India, Pakistan and Afghanistan put together. This Kalinga dynasty had ruled such a large topography for about 800 years. Consistent leadership spanning over hundreds of years. Our Guru this time is the Emperor of Kalingadesam King Satya Gupta.

Satya Gupta was one of the emperors who millions of people looked up to. He ruled them with his love and affection. He was well known for his meticulous planning and his high-profile defence systems. He did invest a major chunk of his resources into the development of his army, procurement of highly effective equipment, welfare of his army men and such.

The emperor's only son Kamala Peeda was a prodigal son. At a very young age, the rumours of his intelligence and leadership skills spread far and wide. He learnt leadership and management from his father's ministers. Most importantly, he spent his evenings with his father as his Guru, learning, discussing, and debating leadership strategies. Satya Gupta was proud of his achievement both as a father and as a Guru. His son will continue the legacy of Kalinga dynasty.

There was one point however, where the father and son disagreed – the country's defence system. Kamala Peeda's stand was that his father was spending way too much into the country's defence. They were a large kingdom with a legacy of sustainable leadership. The chances for an equally powerful enemy waging war against such a kingdom was low. Their dinner time debate on this subject had always ended in disagreement.

At first, Satya Gupta, had relished in his son's capacity to challenge his approach. However, this was getting too far out of hand. Kamala Peeda was convinced that the funding had to be rerouted to other developmental initiatives in the country.

Let's take a pause here.

Reflection Time:

What do you think of Satya Gupta's approach to defence system?

Is Kamala Peeda's judgement fair?

Action Point:

Let's look at your personal defence system now. List your goals that were disturbed or delayed due to your own physical or mental health issues.

Affected goals	How much time was lost? (in hours/days /months/years)	Due to?	Is it body or mind related issue?

Back to the story…

The ongoing conflict ripens, and Satya Gupta wonders how to handover his kingdom to Kamala Peeda when the time comes. He feels like a failure – as a father, as a Guru and as an Emperor. He even consults his ministers and conducts elaborate review together with his son, so he can get a detailed level insight into how the funds are being spent. This attempt only backfires as it further strengthens Kamala Peeda's conviction.

During one of those dinner arguments Kamala Peeda says, "Father, we are such a huge kingdom. No single emperor in this world has the power to rage war against us. Even if someone contrives to do so, then he must join hands with a few other kingdoms and muster up the fleet needed to fight us."

Before Satya Gupta could respond Kamala Peeda continues, "any such huge movement against us will catch wind and we will get to know of that beforehand. We can always pull in our people anytime if there's such a need for war. Why spend our funds on their training and welfare for the whole year!"

At this point, Satya Gupta has nothing more to say. He retreats quietly to his bed chamber.

Let's take a pause here.

Reflection Time:

How will you explain Kamala Peeda the importance of defence?

Action Point:

Can you further elaborate on your health issues categorizing them into repetitive, rare yet critical, rare not critical?

Health Issues	Repetitive/rare yet critical/rare not critical

Back to the story…

King Satya Gupta is unable to sleep though. He thinks long and hard into the last words of his son. Suddenly he gets an idea. He sees that his son is relaxing on the balcony. He walks up to his son holding a large plateful of food.

Kamala Peeda looks at his father with a sigh. "What is this father? Don't you remember that we just had our dinner?"

"Oh! My dear son! This food is not for you. I brought it to the balcony for the birds". Saying so, Satya Gupta places the plate on the balcony railing and starts calling out the birds, making chirping and cooing sounds.

Kamala Peeda wonders in despair. "Father it is late in the evening. This is the time when the birds retreat to their nests. Doesn't matter how much noise you make the birds aren't going to return! The timing isn't right!"

"Exactly! My son!!! This is exactly what I was trying to explain! What if the timing isn't right?" exclaimed Satya Gupta.

Kamala Peeda begins to understand the intension behind his father's actions.

The DEFENCE System:

The defence system isn't anything that can be built impromptu - anytime or anywhere. It needs consistent nurturing and practice, so the system is fully functional to handle any untimely attack.

Action Point:

Let's get smart with our very own defence system now. You have already listed your health challenges in the previous action points. Now it's time to do the following:

- Review these health challenges.
- Get an appointment with your doctor/medical professional.
- Get the necessary tests done to further analyse the weaknesses in your defence system.
- Start working on your well-being today!

In ancient tamil literature there's a saying "Suwar illaamal chittiram varaiya mudiyadhu" meaning "without a wall or a base, paintings cannot be created". Your goals deserve a strong foundation to lean on and that will be your well-being.

Chapter 6

GROWTH MINDSET - BIAS Vs. GOAL

We have laid a strong foundation for our goal and with our well-being in check nothing should go wrong. Is the foundation strong enough? Has bias anything to do with your goals and its foundation? Will bias challenge your foundation? Let's take a strength test.

The Story:

The time machine is taking us to somewhere between the 6th and 5th century BCE to meet our Guru. His name is Siddhartha Gauthama. This is precisely the timeline when Siddhartha Gauthama's name and fame started spreading across the entire Asiatic lands. He travels by foot all the time, trying to spread his knowledge and is always accompanied by many of his disciples. He is yet to be titled "the Buddha". Yes, he is the Guru whose principles millions of people follow even today. His principles and way of life are known to us in the form of Buddhism.

We are still on the timeline where he's travelling relentlessly, spreading his message, despite monsoon weather related hardships. During monsoon season, monks, or sages, usually take to ashrams, temples or any such holy locations wherein there's a possibility of sitting under a roof. At times, the villagers also help such travelling Gurus by giving them temporary accommodation. Siddhartha Gauthama enters a small village with his disciples.

Since the village doesn't have many public places of stay, the villagers agree to help him and his disciples. Each villager agrees to provide at least one monk accommodation. They are all eager to hear this new Guru who is gaining popularity. They extend their full support to Siddhartha Gauthama's retinue. When allotting the accommodations, the villagers realise that they might not have enough space.

"I can help!", comes the voice of a lady from behind, "there's space for one person in my home and I will be happy to share my home with a monk". Complete silence.

Siddhartha Gauthama and his disciples wonder why the villagers are suddenly so quiet. They must be happy to have one more person volunteering space.

The voice that had called out was that of the concubine/prostitute of the village. Women doing prostitution aren't considered a part of the society. They live aloof and aren't welcome to participate in any public or official gathering. It is even considered a sin to step into such a woman's place. One of the villagers gives a quick update to Siddhartha Gauthama on the woman's social status.

"That's very kind of you my lady", responds Siddhartha Gauthama turning to the woman and continues, "one of my disciples will go with you". In a trice, he turns back to the group of his disciples and calls out to one of them saying, "Anantha Theertha, I think you can go with this lady and settle down in the place she provides you".

The crowd is in a state of despair that this new Guru has just directed one of his best disciples to take refuge at a prostitute's home.

Let's take a pause here.

Reflection Time:

What would be the mindset of Siddhartha Gauthama? And his disciple Anantha Theertha?

What do you think will be the mindset of the villagers?

What are your personal thoughts on this situation?

Action Point:

List your personal or group goals that have succeeded due to the involvement of unknown individual(s) or individuals whose cultural/ethnic values are different from that of yours.

Describe the goal	Describe the unexpected success	Who was/were this/these persons(s)?

List your personal or group goals that have been blocked due to a cultural/ethical value mismatch between you and another person(s) whom you had to work with to reach such a goal.

Describe the goal	Describe the blockage due to value mismatch	Who was/were this/these persons(s)?

Back to the story…

The prostitute takes Anantha Theertha to her residence and provides him all the necessities. She sings and dances to entertain her guest in her own way. Anantha Theertha, a well-trained disciple, pays undivided attention to whatever she does.

On the other hand, the villagers start watching the house so attentively, listening to the sounds of music and dance, wondering aloud, "why will a Guru allow such a sinful act!".

Rumours, comments, criticism spread like wildfire. The people even forget that they now have direct access to such a great Guru. What is happening in this 'particular' house becomes the talk of the town gaining more popularity than Siddhartha Gauthama himself. These rumours eventually reach the ears of the Guru, who neither shows any reaction nor has any response to the questions posed by people.

Let's take a pause here.

Reflection Time:

What are your thoughts on this situation?

Action Point:

What is your relationship with your goals? How much does rumours, comments and criticism affect your goal?

Your goal	Describe the rumour/comment/criticism	How much did it affect your goal? Why?

List down any constructive criticism or feedback that has helped you in reaching your goals.

Your goal	Describe the constructive criticism/feedback	How much did it impact your goal? Why?

Back to the story…

The monsoon season is now over. Siddhartha Gauthama and his disciples start making their move out of this village. From the most popular house in the village comes Anantha Theertha to join his Guru. Along with him comes a nun to join Siddhartha Gauthama's journey. She's no other than the lady the villagers had much talked about.

Now Siddhartha Gauthama looks at the villagers and says, "I am walking this path because I see it as the most powerful way to live. But you tell me that her ways are more powerful than mine. Then it only means that I should leave my principles and join her".

He further continues, "It is the intent that matters. My intent is to be DEVOTED to my goal and not get ADDICTED to it."

It is the INTENT that matters:

When one is DEVOTED to his/her goals, one is using strength and valour to help others. On the other hand, when one is ADDICTED to his/her goals, one is using strength and valour to torture and exploit others.

This is the simple yet defining principle behind any developmental situation and/or conflicting situation. BIAS lies right at the roots of the goal's foundation. BIAS has the power to change your relationship with your goals from devotion to addiction.

Action Point:

Review your comments from the last two action points and list your relationship with your goals. Are you devoted or addicted to your goals? why?

Your Goals	Your relationship with goals (devoted/addicted)	Why?

Chapter 7

CRISIS MANAGEMENT

Both your goal and you are now ready to face the brave new world! Once your goal materializes it is not yours anymore. It is a success statement that starts impacting more people.

Wondering who? Just turn back and remind yourself of the people that walked and are walking by you when you were pregnant with your ideas. Family, friends, mentors, colleagues, clients, customers, suppliers, employees - you name it – they have all been there for you and your goal. You notice that so many souls are now either travelling with you/your goal or helping you traverse through it. Will your 'goal boat' sail smoothly through heavy storms? What is your relationship with crisis?

Prelude to the Story:

This story is going to span across chapters 7, 8, 9 and 10.

This time we are going to be transported into another yuga. A yuga is a completely different period or cycle – for example, we know of something called "Ice age" wherein a different set of species had existed. Our time machine is now taking us to Treta Yuga, which had apparently lasted for about 1,296,000 years. This is the period, before the world as we know it, came about.

We are also going to meet many different species. One prominent specie that we will meet is the man-monkey form. We may have learnt that humans are an evolved species. During the time when such an evolution was happening, there were also variants of the evolving species (i.e.) the primary form of monkeys that were able to stand erect - Pithecanthropus erectus or the Homo erectus or the Ape-man. This species was an integral part of our eco-system, as the ape-man was believed to have communicated both with various animals and with human species due to the ability to adjust vocal cords. They are referred to as the VANARAS. NARA means 'man' and VA means 'precursor to'. VANARA(S) refer to the precursor to man.

At times, situations unravel the exceptional actions of certain individuals, and such actions turn out to be demonstrative examples. Therefore, this story is going to present itself with situational Gurus. We will identify them along the way.

The Story:

The Kingdom of Bharatha (mostly today's Indian sub-continent) is in a moment of celebration. The crown prince Rama's coronation is scheduled for the next day. He is destined to be the ruler of the nation and has been preparing himself all his life. However, due to an unexpected turn of events, mostly internal politics, he and his wife Sita, and his younger brother Lakshmana, are sent to exile for 14 years, just a few hours before the coronation was to take place.

Rama, Lakshmana, and Sita are to leave all the luxuries and live incognito in the deep dark forests. They connect more deeply with nature, adapt to various situations and flow along with nature. 13 years pass by. They are looking forward to spending the last year in peace, successfully completing the exile period, and returning home to their loved ones. Rama will finally get his chance to become the King of Bharatha.

On one such day, filled with hope, when Rama and Lakshmana were hunting for their food, they hear the noise of Sita. They come rushing to the spot only to find that she has been abducted. The trio had learned to be in a state of crisis for 13 years. However, this abduction left Rama totally depressed. Where to find her? How to find her? Is she dead or alive?

Though they were the young princes of Bharatha, they cannot leverage their own army for the search operation. It is as per the rules of the exile that they are never to use any of their princely resources. Wandering in the forest in search of Sita, Rama and Lakshmana enter Kishkindha, the kingdom of ape-men. They meet their leader Sugreeva, who seemed to have lost his kingdom and was in the lookout for someone with sharp combat strategies. He had an army of ape-men called the Vanar-sena at his disposal.

Rama and Lakshmana strike a deal with Sugreeva that they will support him with the strategies needed to regain his lost kingdom after which he needs to support them with his resources for their 'search for Sita operation'.

Let's take a pause here.

Reflection Time:

What would be the mindset of Rama? What would be the mindset of Sita? What are your thoughts on the crisis?

Action Point:

List the crisis situations you have faced or are going through in life and reflect on how you have handled/are handling them.

Crisis	Period	How have you handled it?

Back to the story…

As the relationship between Rama, Lakshmana, and Sugreeva develops, more information about the abduction starts presenting itself. A group of Vanaras (i.e.) the Vanar-sena, had seen a Pushpaka Vimaana (aircraft) moving above their terrain in the south-east direction. This aircraft looked like a flying chariot and was flying so low that the Vanaras could get a better view from the treetops. Furthermore, this aircraft seemed luxurious and from it came the crying sounds of a lady. The lady threw one of her earrings and one of her bangles out of the aircraft. They had an inkling that this could be the abduction of a queen, princess, or the like. They jumped around and tried to follow the vehicle as much as they could and had picked up the jewels that fell from it. The pieces of jewellery had a mark of royalty, which they couldn't identify though. So, they had retained it safely, to possibly hand it over to anyone that comes enquiring of such abduction.

When they showed the jewellery, Rama confirmed it to be Sita's jewellery. During the abduction, Sita had tried to send a last message to her husband – she was alive and conscious at the time of abduction, and she'd been abducted by someone who was probably wealthy/powerful, and he'd taken her somewhere south-east. There's hope.

As agreed, Rama and Lakshmana help Sugreeva in winning his kingdom back. King Sugreeva now splits his Vanar-sena into groups and deploys them in all directions to be 100% sure that no stone is left unturned in the search process. He puts together the best of the best team to travel south-east, which is possibly the zone where Lady Sita could be.

Let's take a pause here.

Reflection Time:

What are your thoughts on both Rama's and Sita's approach to crisis?

Action Point:

Are there any patterns or connections between those crisis situations that you had listed in the previous action point? If yes, please list them here. Also list the patterns/connections in your approach to such situations.

List patterns/connections between crisis situations:

1.

2.

3.

4.

5.

List patterns/connections in your approach

1.

2.

3.

4.

5.

Back to the story…

The group of Vanaras that had headed south-east have been running around ransacking every possible spot in their vicinity but in vain. Tired and exhausted they take shelter in a cave to recuperate. Sampathi, an old eagle who also happens to be there, overhears their conversation, and enquires about their mission. He is touched by the plight of the Vanar-sena and decides to help. Using his visionary skills, he guesstimates that a lady of similar description is probably there in the direction that they are looking for.

Sampathi adds that the possible location is not within the precincts of Bharatha, it is rather further down south – in Lanka (today's Sri Lanka). From the spot where they are to the spot where the Lady could be, he further guesstimates, as 100 yojanas (1 yojana = 10 miles).

Even if there is a remote possibility that Sampathi's predictions are true, the Vanar-sena will leave no stones unturned. However, for the entire team to process such data, it means at least one of them will have to travel across the ocean and confirm Lady Sita's presence. They look at each other in confusion, discuss and debate all possibilities and options. They finally identify and deploy the ideal resource for this task – HANUMAN.

… to be continued in chapter 8.

Internalising the Crisis:

Crisis are either situations that strike us when we are unaware or situations that have been growing slowly and gradually metamorphosize into something unbearable. However different each of our crisis experiences are, one common denominator is that we are deprived of essential resources to handle them. We feel crippled and caged.

Our situational Gurus, Rama and Sita were fully aware of the lack of external resources. What they did differently was to internalize. When one is internalizing, one is using the internal resources or the inner strength to fight the odds and really look at what is practically possible that very moment.

Lady Sita used the last ounce of her inner strength to communicate with her husband in whichever way possible. Rama, on the other hand, realized that whatever was to come, would be huge and he needed to muster up the resources. Using his inner strength (i.e.) war strategies, he decided to help King Sugreeva and strike a deal for the much-needed resources. They both never gave up.

Internalizing helps you to turn the pain into power, eliminates the fear, builds zero-tolerance to distraction, and helps one to never give up. Every situation is unique, even if many are going through a similar crisis such as a pandemic or a war, each of our experiences will be unique. There cannot be any comparison between crises or individual experiences. The only parameter we can work on, is our individual internal approach and this comes with practice.

Action Point:

If given a second chance, how or what would your approach be?

Choose any one of your crisis experiences and share your thoughts on internalization it.

Describe the crisis	
Your previous approach	
Given a 2nd chance how will you turn the pain into power?	

How will you eliminate the fear and develop zero-tolerance to any distractions?	
What do you think the outcome will be when you create the "never-give-up" attitude?	
Summarize the internal resources you will deploy	

Chapter 8

CONFLICT MANAGEMENT & DECISION MAKING

Withering storms come with practice. Your goals and your mindset are gaining strength with each day of effort that you are putting in. You have been shaping your goal with precise purpose(s)- having a vision for your goal, understanding your stakeholders, understanding your relationship with crisis, bias and anger as well as understanding your defence system- after going through several tests both internally and externally in nature.

However, strengths can turn into weaknesses when there's a lack of flexibility and spontaneity. How flexible are you? How spontaneous are you when it comes to some critical decision making? Let's find out.

Back to the story…

We are continuing with the same story from Treta yuga. The search operation for Lady Sita is in full swing. The Vanar-sena team that was responsible for the south-east direction has stumbled upon a clue. They aren't sure of it yet. Hence, they have just identified a leader for this task – Hanuman, who is also one of the ape-men.

There is so much hope vested in Hanuman. He is one among them. Yet, there's some attributes in him that are distinctive. He possesses the ability to resize himself (i.e.) he can become a small little monkey jumping around the trees or expand in size and move a mountain, if needed. He also possesses the wit to assume any capacity or activity provided to him and do the same with enthusiasm.

The brief given to him is to cross the ocean, find out if Lady Sita is in Lanka and come back to report within a day. Until his name was called out, Hanuman hadn't thought of it. This was an unexpected role and responsibility. Hanuman considers this task for a while and breaks it down even further:

- Jump and cross approximately 100 yojanas (i.e.) 1000 miles or 1600 kilometres,
- Pinpoint exact location of Lady Sita,
- Is she alive? If yes, in what condition is she?
- Communicate to Lady Sita that a rescue operation is in progress,
- Survey the enemy,
- Warn the enemy,
- Complete all these tasks within a day.

Let's take a pause here.

Reflection Time:

What are your thoughts on Hanuman's mindset? What are your thoughts on assuming unexpected roles and responsibilities?

Action Point:

How many times have you assumed spontaneous roles and responsibilities? Or entered the no-man's zone? Was it the conflicts within such a zone or the decision making that was challenging?

List such experiences here.

Unexpected roles or responsibilities	Timespan (in days /months/years)	What was most challenging? (conflicts/decision making/ other)

Back to the story…

Hanuman decides to proceed with his task. Goes on top of a mountain and resizes himself adequately that his body can wither the mighty ocean. He takes a deep breath and reminds himself of Rama, visualizes Rama meeting Sita and being happy, and builds up the enthusiasm needed for this task. He now puts his undivided attention on the task and takes a big leap.

On the way to his goal, Hanuman faces some roadblocks.

The first one comes a short while after Hanuman makes his big leap. Suddenly, out of the ocean a huge land mass starts emerging. Mainaaka mountain creeps out of the waters almost blocking the way of Hanuman and says, "hey dear monkey, you seem to be jumping in full force. However, this is a vast ocean, and you are bound to get tired soon. Won't you just sit on me and rest for a while?"

"Dear mountain, this is very kind of you to have shown your concern for me. Your kind words have removed my tiredness. I already feel like I have rested in your shades for a while. I am on a mission. I promise to pay you a visit when I am done with my mission". Saying so, Hanuman gives a big hug to Mainaaka mountain and continues his journey towards Lanka.

After a few yojanas, he sees some strong tidal movement in the ocean. The snake queen Surasa opens her huge hood raising from the ocean and stopping Hanuman. "Hey monkey! I have a boon that you will enter my mouth today! There's no other way out!"

"Is that so?" says Hanuman, "don't you think I am a little too big for your mouth?"

"Well, I can always increase the size of my mouth", says Surasa hissing and further expanding her large hood.

Hanuman immediately decides to increase his size. Surasa doesn't give up either. In the fight for increasing the size, the snake queen wins, opening her mouth, clouding the whole skyline.

Hanuman resizes himself into a small little monkey in a trice, enters her mouth and exits it saying, "well, I have now entered your mouth! So, your boon is fulfilled! Bye!!!!"

Hanuman is so close to the land of Lanka when the demoness Simhika appears from nowhere. She also tries to scare him away and threatens to eat him up. The resizing game begins between the two. When Simhika's mouth is large enough, Hanuman enters. This time however, he decides to resize himself inside her mouth, expanding himself in a way that he breaks her skull open, leaving her dead in the ocean.

When Hanuman enters the landscape of Lanka, he resizes himself into a small monkey so he can roam around being invisible. Lankini, the fortress guard, takes note of this unusual monkey movement and stops him, "who are you?"

"I am new to this place", says Hanman switching his vocal cord to speak, "I think this is a beautiful land, if you permit me, I want to just do some sightseeing and I will get back to you in a trice!"

"A speaking monkey!", wonders Lankini, "what business will you have in this land?", sensing something unexpected is in the making, "as a guard for this place, I cannot allow you to enter".

Hanuman resizes himself adequately to kick her out of his way, yet not killing her, and proceeds into the city.

… to be continued in chapter 9.

Reflection Time:

What do you think were the differences between these roadblocks/conflicts that Hanuman had faced? Share your reflection on Hanuman's approach?

Hanuman's approach to resolving conflicts:

Delving a little deeper into the conflicts and our situational Guru - Hanuman's approach, the metaphors can be further elaborated in the following manner:

Roadblock (metaphor)	Decoding the metaphor	Hanuman's approach	Technique used to resolve conflicts
The Mainaaka mountain	Nature, a conflict with nature arising out of care and concern	Resolve the conflict through discussion	Showing love and acknowledging the concern
The Snake queen Surasa	Nature, a friend posing as an enemy again out of care and concern	Resolve the conflict using tactical approach	Intelligence or commonsense
The demoness Simhika	Unknown element, threat/enemy	Resolve the conflict by eliminating the enemy	Using force
The fortress guard Lankini	A responsible officer on duty in the opponent's land, a possible threat	Resolve the conflict by displacing the threat temporarily. Eliminating this threat will attract unnecessary attention a little too early, derailing Hanuman from the primal mission.	Using a combination of intelligence and mild force

The 4 pillars of success:

DHRUTHI – DHRUSHTI – MATHI – DAAKSHYAM

Lord Hanuman, commonly known as the monkey-God, is the God that people in some parts of the world pray to when they must focus on something, win a game, write an exam, prepare for a job interview or the like. When you ask them why they are praying to such a monkey-God, the most common explanation is that praying to him gives them the strength to succeed.

An ape-man from Treta yuga transcending millions of years is celebrated and prayed to, even today. This is because he is the symbol of success. The reason is he, by his actions, has demonstrated the 4 pillars of success in conflict management and decision making. Lord Hanuman is a visual form of this ideology DHRUTHI, DHRUSHTI, MATHI and DAAKSHYAM. These four pillars, if implemented effectively, always results in success.

PILLARS of success	**Meaning**	**Hanuman's approach to conflict management & decision making**
DHRUTHI	Stability, Determination	He demonstrates stability, determination in his approach in every situation, however unexpected it might be.
DHRUSHTI	Focus, Vision	He demonstrates focus on the primal mission and hence he can take quick decisions on how to approach each of the conflicts. Whether discussing, debating, or eliminating the conflict, he never prioritized his personal ego. How will such discussion or elimination impact the goal? He focuses only on the goal.
MATHI	Intelligence, Commonsense	He demonstrates intelligence in identifying the type of conflict and applying flexible approach each time. This capacity to resize himself – he does use it but not according to his own will, rather according to the situation that unfolds.
DAAKSHYAM	Resourcefulness	He demonstrates resourcefulness from the very minute this task gets assigned to him. The briefing of the task vs. his own assessment of the task, stands proof on how resourceful he wants to be. He doesn't want to come back with just the update on Lady Sita. He wants to produce a full report - SWOT of the opponent, communicate hope to Lady Sita and warn the opponent, to also give the opponent a last chance, so a war can be avoided.

Lord Hanuman's ability to resize himself, his ultimate flexibility runs throughout these four pillars of success. Is it still possible in today's world? Yes, the mind can be resized, the ego can be resized anytime to adapt to each situation and demonstrate flexibility.

When you demonstrate stability, determination in the processes, prioritizing the goal/vision each time you take a decision, use your intelligence, your commonsense in accessing each situation, being flexible in resolving conflicts, demonstrate resourcefulness in going above and beyond expectations then success is inevitable.

Action Point:

From the previous action point, pick out the most challenging conflict and/or decision you had to handle. Given a 2nd chance, what will your approach be considering Hanuman's ideology.

PILLARS of success	**Meaning**	**How will you change your approach?**	**What will be the potential impact?**
DHRUTHI	Stability, Determination		
DHRUSHTI	Focus, Vision		
MATHI	Intelligence, Commonsense		
DAAKSHYAM	Resourcefulness		

Chapter 9

COMMUNICATION & RELATIONSHIP MANAGEMENT

Your goals and mindset are now loaded with effective tools that will help you in traversing through crises and conflicts and be an effective decision maker. Your 'goal boat' has now turned into a huge Noah's ark, holding so many stakeholders that are relying upon your mission. Will they still stick around while you wither each crisis and conflict? Are these relationships hanging by the thread or are they clinging on to an iron rod? Or do we have a fully functional two-way road for communication?

Back to the story…

Hanuman has entered the land of Lanka successfully. He begins the search operation immediately. At the same time, he reviews each location, the strength of the forts, the wealth of the city and its people, the volume of security, the abundance of resources. He looks around every place where women are gathered in search of Lady Sita.

He arrives at the large palace of King of Lanka – Ravana. King Ravana is known to have 10 heads. His intelligence, power, wealth, and arrogance are known far and wide. Hanuman notices the Pushpaka Vimana (aircraft) that was used in the process of abduction. If this is the same aircraft that the Vanaras had seen, then he is at the precincts of the potential opponent. Hanuman decides to take a sneak peek at Ravana's lifestyle.

Resizing himself into a tiny monkey, he goes around observing the lengths and breaths of the palace. He sneaks quietly into Ravana's bed chamber. Ravana is sleeping. Hanuman comes close to him and watches him attentively. He looks around the room. There's left over food, wine, and many women – possibly captives lying drunk, in the room. Hanuman realises that it isn't the first time Ravana has abducted anyone. There are possibly many more captives in and around the palace. No sign of Lady Sita's presence yet.

She is certainly not inside the palace. Hanuman leaves the palace quietly. He sees a park close to the palace, finds a branch to hop onto, reaches the top to look around. He settles down quietly, feeling lost. So much effort and such great risks taken. What if Ravana has killed Lady Sita already? Everything becomes pointless if this is the case.

Hanuman has the capacity to rejuvenate and motivate himself, by visualizing. He does so, imagining all the good times that will embrace the land of Bharatha when Rama and Sita are reunited and take over as king and queen. He prays that Lady Sita would show herself to him. The moment he opens his eyes, he notices a crying woman sitting under the very same tree that he is in.

Let's take a pause here.

Reflection Time:

What are your thoughts on this situation? Should Hanuman be communicating with this woman? If so, how?

Action Point:

Hanuman is actively observing the situation first before communicating. Reflect on the number of times/situations wherein your observations have supported you in effective communication.

Situation	Your observations prior to communication	How has the observation helped you in communicating effectively?

Back to the story…

Hanuman continues observing this lady, looking for traces of resemblance to the description provided by Rama. This lady looks like she has not eaten in a while. Her old clothes and overall condition, gives the impression that she might have been in this state for a while. He notices a single bangle and earring, lying close to her on the ground. This could be her. However, these pieces of jewellery need to be observed more closely for the royal markings.

It is pre-dawn, and the park is completely deserted. This could be the right time to approach this woman.

There's some noise coming from the palace though. Ravana has woken up and he is on his way to the park with his retinue. He walks in front of this woman and starts speaking to her threateningly.

"All of the women that have been abducted, have given into my needs, and surrendered. They are living a happy and luxurious life because of me!", exclaimed Ravana. "Your husband is a nobody. He had already lost his kingdom and was roaming in the forests when I found you. Who knows whether he is still alive or dead!"

The woman is crying profusely now.

"I will give you a couple of months. If you do not oblige, I shall kill you and feed your body to the animals!"

The crying woman starts speaking, "My husband is a noble man. He will keep his promises. He will come for me no matter what the situation is".

She further continues in her weak yet stubborn tone, "when he comes, I expect that you hold his hands, become friends with him and return me safely to him!"

Ravana roars in anger and abuses her verbally. He orders his retinue to talk some sense into this woman and storms out of the park.

His guards or the ogresses use a different style of approach.

"Ravana is a mighty king. He will make you the queen of all queens, if you just agree to his wishes", they begin coaxing her. "It has been so many months since you have arrived here. Still no sign of your husband. What if something had really happened to him!"

"Let's say for your sake that he is alive and is coming for you," they continue their negative talk, "do you think he has the resources to fight a mighty king such as Ravana? He is sure to get killed within minutes!"

The woman does not respond. Her crying continues.

After a while, the retinue leaves her alone, giving her a break from the verbal torture.

Hanuman, sitting on the top of his tree, is keenly observing everything that is being said and done and beyond.

Quick Reflection:

How would you describe Ravana's communication?

Form of Communication	Language of Communication	Tone of Communication	Message

How would you describe the guards/ogresses' communication?

Form of Communication	Language of Communication	Tone of Communication	Message

How would you describe Sita's communication?

Form of Communication	Language of Communication	Tone of Communication	Message

When the whole park quietens, the woman gets up. One can clearly see how depressed she is. It looks like she is considering suicide by hanging herself. She is about to bend one of the branches.

Hanuman decides it is the right time for communication. He first switches his vocal cord to speak the human language and starts narrating a story, without making any move from the treetop.

The woman hears somebody speaking and listens carefully. Is it one of the guards or ogresses? Or Ravana himself? No, this voice is different! She pays attention.

Hanuman begins narrating the story of a prince and princess, how they had to leave their kingdom to live in a forest and how the princess was snatched away from the prince.

"Who is that?!" wonders the woman aloud, "Who is narrating my own life story to me?"

Hanuman further continues the story and explains how Rama and Lakshmana ended up meeting King Sugreeva, how they helped him get his kingdom and how they planned a search and rescue mission for his dear wife Sita.

"This part of the story is new!" wonders Sita, "Who are you? Will you present yourself before me? Or continue to be in hiding?"

"I am the messenger of Shri Rama and one of the army men/Vanara from King Sugreeva's Vanar-sena, my Lady", says Hanuman climbing slowly down the tree.

Hanuman now presents the "Kanaiyaazhi" the royal ring of Rama, filling in the rest of the details.

As the discussion progresses, Lady Sita begins to understand that he is somebody genuine and has no relationship to her abductor.

"How did a small monkey like you, manage to cover the entire seascape and reach this far?" wonders Sita.

Hanuman now shows his ability to resize. He also offers her the possibility that he could carry her on his shoulders and get her swiftly to her husband.

The determined queen-to-be of Bharatha, Lady Sita, is clear that her husband must arrive and set things right, meeting his opponent in person. She is not the only woman that was abducted. There are many other lives trapped in here that deserve to be freed. She further shares her observations on Ravana, his guards, his strengths, and his weaknesses and her understanding of the landscape, seascape and distances between both the land masses.

Hanuman instils hope in her. She needs to stay put until Rama, Lakshmana, Sugreeva, and his whole army (the Vanar-sena) arrive in Lanka.

Quick Reflection:

How would you describe Hanuman's communication?

Form of Communication	Language of Communication	Tone of Communication	Message

How would you describe Sita's communication?

Form of Communication	Language of Communication	Tone of Communication	Message

Hanuman now moves on to his next task. Attracting attention.

He creates a ruckus in the park demolishing and destructing whatever or whoever comes his way. The whole army of Ravana are now desperate to kill this unknown monkey that is resizing himself all the time and continuing his destruction.

Disturbed, Ravana sends some of his ministers and important men, only to see them get killed by this ape-man. One of his own sons get killed by Hanuman. It is time they pulled this ape-man into Ravana's court, so they can find out exactly who he is and what he wants.

They somehow manage to bring Hanuman into Ravana's court. Hanuman uses his tail as a cushion and seats himself right in front of Ravana. He introduces himself as the messenger of Shri Rama, a Vanara from the Vanar-sena of King Sugreeva. He further goes on to give an account of his observations of Lanka – a SWOT of Ravana vs. a SWOT of Rama, Lakshmana, King Sugreeva, and their retinue. He warns Ravana that if he doesn't handover Lady Sita safely to Rama, a war is inevitable, underpinning the consequences.

Some of Ravana's ministers and even his eldest son, advise him many times to reconsider his stand. Ravana, being arrogant in his approach, chooses not to listen to any such suggestions, abuses Hanuman, and sets fire to his tail as a warning to Rama. Hanuman uses the fire as an opportunity to set the entire fortress ablaze, reverberating the warning message and leaves Lanka.

… to be continued in Chapter 10.

Quick Reflection:

How would you describe Hanuman's actions and communication?

Form of Communication	Language of Communication	Tone of Communication	Message

How would you describe Ravana's actions and communication?

Form of Communication	Language of Communication	Tone of Communication	Message

The 4 pillars of effective communication:

Ravana sticks to a single form, tone, and language of communication, which is mostly a monologue. There's no relationship management strategy involved in his approach.

Hanuman chooses an indirect form of communication, while speaking to Lady Sita in a polite tone, steadily delivering her life story, as a mechanism to stop her from committing suicide. He doesn't show his capabilities or offer support, until he gains her trust. The key message to be delivered to her was HOPE, which was delivered after the relationship is established.

Sita delivers her message to her husband via Hanuman. She points out the actions needed and the challenges ahead. She takes time to first understand who this visitor is and once the trust relationship is established, her communication is direct, clear, and concise. The key message is DIRECT ACTION against the opponent to save not just her, but also to save many more captives.

Hanuman chooses the direct form of communication when speaking to Ravana, leaving no cards unturned, also leaving the option open for a truce, so a cordial relationship may be maintained between two kingdoms in the future. When Ravana does not respond accordingly, he delivers his key message, which is WARNING Ravana of the consequences.

The bedrock of effective communication is OBSERVATION. Both our situational Gurus - Hanuman and Lady Sita, had used their observations effectively. Hence, it was a spontaneous action for them to choose the right form, language, tone and message, every time. When one is using observation, the communication naturally gravitates to being fact-based, which makes even the most difficult conversation effective.

<table>
<tr><td>RIGHT FORM</td><td>RIGHT LANGUAGE</td></tr>
<tr><td colspan="2">OBSERVATION</td></tr>
<tr><td>RIGHT TONE</td><td>RIGHT MESSAGE</td></tr>
</table>

Action Point:

Pick one situation from your previous action points. Given a 2nd chance, how will you use your observations effectively? What will the form, language, tone, and message be?

Describe the situation briefly:	
Describe your observations briefly:	

Form of Communication	Language of Communication	Tone of Communication	Message
YOUR EARLIER APPROACH			
Form of Communication	Language of Communication	Tone of Communication	Message
YOUR NEW APPROACH			

Chapter 10

SUSTAINABLE RESOURCE MANAGEMENT

Manoeuvring through internal and external challenges, your goal is growing stronger. This book will have its ending. However, your goal and your growth mindset must go on! It is time to think about sustainability. How sustainable is your goal and its peripherals?

Back to the story…

Operation 'search Sita' is complete. The victorious Hanuman reports all the proceedings to Rama immediately upon seeing him. Based on the update provided, Sugreeva's resources are now deployed. Other animals in the forest also join forces to support Rama on his mission. It is evident that all these resources cannot be transported via air to Lanka. Hence, they all decide to build a bridge connecting the lands Bharatha and Lanka.

They identify the closest land mass from where the bridge could be built and get started with the task. Moving boulders and rocks into the seascape, the Vanara-sena, together with the help of all the animals, build a bridge. This bridge will be remembered by history as the Rama Sethu or Rama's bridge. Traces of this bridge can even be found today.

Note: This bridge is also called Adam's bridge. It is approximately a 48 kilometres long chain of natural limestone shoals between Pamban Island, the south-east coast of modern-day India and Mannar Island, the north-west coast of modern-day Sri Lanka. Researchers are studying this bridge, and its evolution.

Let's take a pause here.

Reflection Time:

What is your relationship with nature?

Action Point:

Identify at least 3 natural resources that you use every day. Can you estimate how much of it you need every day?

3 Natural Resources used every day	Usage in litres/kilos/any other measuring scale applicable

Back to the story…

All the animals put in their best efforts to build this bridge. Certainly, there were strong and heavy built animals moving the large rocks and boulders together with the Vanara-sena. There were also small animals and birds contributing. Slowly and steadily, a strong bridge was being established. The entire gamut of the animal kingdom was supporting Rama in his mission to establish a bridge reaching Lanka. This was just the first step. There's a war awaiting.

Rama makes a stop here. He considers it important to appreciate the efforts of all the animals that have helped him complete this first phase of the mission. He settles down on a rock and first thanks the squirrel for all his efforts. The Vanara-sena wonders why Rama should choose to start with a small, little squirrel.

Rewarding and recognizing his resources at every stage of progress was always important for Rama. He explains to the curious Vanara-sena, that the squirrel has contributed to this task equally, putting in his fullest effort and capabilities.

Let's take a pause here.

Reflection Time:

What do you think of Rama's approach to rewarding and recognizing? How different or similar is your approach to rewarding?

Action Point:

List the 3 most important resources contributing to your goal. How do you recognize them?

The 3 most important resources	Your Rewards & Recognition approach

List the 3 least important resources contributing to your goal. How do you recognize them?

3 least important resources	Your Rewards & Recognition approach

Back to the story…

Rama, Lakshmana, Sugreeva, Hanuman, and their retinue of Vanara-sena's, surprise the unassuming army of Ravana. Their methods are driven by their natural instincts. Each animal uses his or her strengths both internally and externally to fight for their mission. Ravana's losses are heavy, which leaves Lanka devastated. Eventually, Ravana also meets his end at the hands of Rama.

The War is over.

Rama is elated to be united with his wife Sita. However, he is fully aware that the outcome of a war is savage destruction. He still has a lot of responsibilities to carry out.

He frees all the women that were trapped in the palaces and various locations in Lanka. Provides them an opportunity to safely return to their own homes or move on to a safer place to restart their lives with dignity.

The king of the country is dead. Rama never indulged in the war to crown himself the king of this land. He will soon be leaving for his own kingdom. Hence, he identifies Vibhishana, the younger brother of Ravana, to be the King of Lanka. Vibhishana was one amongst the many ministers, who had tried their best to stop Ravana from committing grave sins. Rama supports Vibhishana in rebuilding his Kingdom.

Once all tasks in Lanka are done, Rama thanks Sugreeva for all his support and hands over his Varana-sena. Hanuman chooses to be with Rama, Sita, and Lakshmana for the rest of his life.

Rama further ensures that the animals that had supported him in his mission, return safely to nature.

On completing the 14 years of exile, Rama, Sita, Lakshmana, and Hanuman return to the Kingdom of Bharatha to commence the "Rama Rajya" – Rama's reign.

Jai Shri Ram!!!

The 3 Mantras for sustainable resource management:

GROWTH PLAN – REPLACEMENT PLAN – EXIT PLAN

Our situational Guru - Rama's approach to the war and Lanka, demonstrates the presence of these 3 mantras.

- In freeing the captives and providing them with an opportunity to live with dignity, he created a growth plan.
- In identifying an appropriate leader to take over as the ruler, he brought about a replacement plan.
- In supporting the newly formed kingdom to be rebuilt, and handing over all resources, he demonstrated his exit plan.

When we respect the goals and mindsets of the resources that are contributing to our goal, we become sustainable leaders.

Action Point:

Let's do a sustainability checklist for your goal right now!

GROWTH PLAN

How many resources do you have? What will be your growth plan for them?

Type of resources	Growth Plan

REPLACEMENT PLAN

How many natural resources do you need for your goal to succeed? What is your replacement plan?

Type of natural resources	Replacement Plan

EXIT PLAN

What will be your exit plan when your goals are consummated?

1.

2.

3.

4.

5.

CONCLUSION

This has been a long journey back in time. You have met so many gurus that have shown you their yogic way to changing your mindset, building a growth mindset, and fine tuning your goals. Let's do a quick recap the yogic way, which is starting with a story.

The Story:

In all these periods and the places, we have just travelled to, the Gurukul style of education was prominent. A certain yogi, sage, or Guru took some shishyas or students as their responsibility. These students left their own families and lived/travelled with their Gurus all the time.

There were 64 forms of art or subjects that were imparted. Their learnings involved gardening, cooking, natural and medicinal sciences, meditation, yogic practices, mathematics, geography, history, art of warfare, politics, leadership and management strategies, creative work, poetry, languages, music, dance and much more. The focus was to gain a basic understanding of all 64 subjects. Then the students chose to gain expertise on some of the subjects that they wanted to learn more.

The way of imparting education was similar to that of the preparation of medicines. The Gurus used herbs and plants to make medicines. They were fully aware of the sharp tastes of the herbs. So, they always coated the medicines with honey, sugar, or such like substances, that made such medicines consumable. Similarly, the core concepts that needed to be imparted in their education was also sugar-coated in the form of stories. This storytelling or story-boarding approach helped their students remember heavy concepts, easily.

The Gurus responsibility does not end with imparting training or education to a select few. The knowledge must be passed on to generations. Carvings on the stones or walls of temples and other public buildings, were the first form of visual storyboarding that was used. With time, palm leaves were used as booklets and the Gurus wrote the key concepts on them and saved them in repositories or libraries.

The Gurus were guardians of knowledge. When kingdoms clashed and war breaks-out, the first chosen places for destruction by the enemies are unfortunately, temples, public buildings, and libraries. When houses or farmlands are destroyed, people will always find a way to rebuild. When knowledge is destroyed, it can stall the growth of any nation for many years, even centuries. Knowing that knowledge will always be a vulnerable target, our Gurus created sugar-coated, fun-filled stories that can be easily told to children. These stories can travel beyond centuries to enlighten future generations.

When the needed education is imparted, it is time for convocation. This convocation is basically a short recap of all the aspects of their education. The Guru briefly discussed every topic and ended each discussion point with "SWADHYAYE PRAVACCHANAM CHA" which broadly means, to keep on "learning and sharing knowledge".

Convocation Time:

Following this lineage of Gurus and trusting in their recipe, this book carries the short forms of 10 such storylines that show the future generation how to build a sustainable growth mindset and traverse through change.

1. In our first chapter we met a Guru who removed the Ghevada creeper at the house of a poor man pushing him out of his comfort zone. The poor man further removed its roots, to begin thinking out of the box. He does so with a detached attachment and ultimately finds the gold pot. *SWADHYAYE PRAVACCHANAM CHA*
2. The Guru from our second chapter played with a piece of jewellery, did a thorough analysis of the status of the kingdom and its people, and finally made the ambitious king realise the difference between having a goal with and without purpose. *SWADHYAYE PRAVACCHANAM CHA*
3. In the third chapter, our angry Guru Kaushika learns that anger is the showstopper to success when he goes to Mithila city and meets Dharmavyadha the divine butcher. *SWADHYAYE PRAVACCHANAM CHA*
4. By challenging a successful farmer, asking him to cut down his crops, the Guru from our fourth chapter helped us understand the importance of Vision and relationship with stakeholders. *SWADHYAYE PRAVACCHANAM CHA*
5. In the fifth chapter, we travelled to Kalingadesam and met Satya Gupta, who was not only the Guru, but also the father of Kamala Peeda. Satya Gupta helped us understand the importance of a fully functional defence system (i.e.) our well-being. *SWADHYAYE PRAVACCHANAM CHA*
6. The sixth chapter carried us all the way to meet Gauthama Buddha who helped us understand our relationship with BIAS and its eventual influence on our goals. *SWADHYAYE PRAVACCHANAM CHA*
7. The seventh chapter took us all the way to Treta Yuga, to meet Rama, Lakshmana, and Sita, who were going through several phases of crises', to understand how internal strengths can be leveraged to manage a crisis. *SWADHYAYE PRAVACCHANAM CHA*

8. The eight chapter introduced us to this impromptu leader, Hanuman, who used his Druthi (determination), Drushti (focus), Mathi (intelligence) and Dakshyam (resourcefulness) to manage various conflicts and take decisions effectively. *SWADHYAYE PRAVACCHANAM CHA*
9. In the ninth chapter, we further saw the communication between Sita and Hanuman, Ravana and Sita, Hanuman, and Ravana, to understand both effective and ineffective communication. Sita and Hanuman, used their observations as the cornerstone to help them choose the right tone, form, language and message in communicating effectively. *SWADHYAYE PRAVACCHANAM CHA*
10. In the tenth chapter, we saw how Rama rewarded or recognised his resources at every stage of progress, and most importantly understood the role of a growth plan, replacement plan, and exit plan in any mission. *SWADHYAYE PRAVACCHANAM CHA*

This concept of storytelling and passing on knowledge is prevalent across the globe amongst almost all the cultures. We have graded them as mythological stories and boxed them into Greek mythology, Norse mythology, Chinese mythology, Indian mythology and so on. These are pearls of wisdom awaiting to be unleashed. We may already have the key to unlock a sustainable world. We just need to start using it.

Action Point:

This book is inspired by many voluminous books, scriptures, and stories. This is a light and short version of the yogic way or the sustainable way to change mindset. It is, therefore, only a small window to the abundance of knowledge. How will you continue learning and sharing knowledge?

List the next 5 books you will read and why?

Name of the Books	Why will you read? What is your aim?

List the next 5 persons/groups you will share this knowledge with and how?

Name of the persons/groups	**How do you plan to share the knowledge?**

Bibliography

1. Guru Charitra: The two incarnations of Lord Dattatreya - Edited and revised by Dr.V.R.Prabhu

2. Manasvi (Volumes 1 & 2): The art of mind management through Sundara Kaanda by Rallabandi Srirama Chakradha, Davuluri Madhavi, and Amara Sarada Deepthi

3. A systematic course in the ancient tantric techniques of Yoga and Kriya by Swami Satyananda Saraswati

4. Sanskrit Language Teachings by the Central Sanskrit University (Formerly Rashtriya Sanskrit Sansthan), deemed to be University, under the ministry of education, Government of India.

5. The Theory and Practice of Change Management by John Hayes

6. The Effective Change Manager's Handbook: Essential Guidance to the Change Management Body of Knowledge by Richard Smith, David King et al.

Video References:

1. Story of Dharmavyadha by Ananda Sangha Worldwide : https://www.youtube.com/watch?v=VffQqTM5i04
2. Hanuman Chalisa: Secrets Revealed by Om Dhumatkar https://www.youtube.com/watch?v=bEFgf0NIjak
3. Sundara Kandam Sri.U.Ve.Velukkudi Krishnan Swami Discourse in Tamil https://www.youtube.com/watch?v=OVtM1P3iBwc&t=3573s

Glossary

Abduction	the action of taking someone away by force or deception
Ablaze	burning fiercely
Acclimated	to adapt (someone) to a new temperature, altitude, climate, environment, or situation
Accolades	an award or privilege granted as a special honour or as an acknowledgement of merit
Agitated	nervous because of worry or fear that is difficult
Anticipate	to take action in preparation for something that you think will happen
Appalling	inspiring horror, dismay, or disgust
Astonished	greatly surprised or impressed; amazed
Balcony railing	A rail is a horizontal bar/wall/structure attached to posts or fixed round the edge of something as a fence or support
Barefoot	without wearing anything on the feet
Boon	something that is very helpful and improves the quality of life, a timely benefit or a blessing
Boulders	A large rock, typically one that has been worn smooth by erosion. In geology, a boulder (or rarely bowlder) is a rock fragment with size greater than 25.6 centimetres (10.1 in) in diameter.
Captive	a person or animal whose ability to move or act freely is limited by being kept in a space; a prisoner, especially a person held by the enemy during a war
Chaotic	in a state of complete confusion and disorder
Circulatory	relating to the system that moves blood through the body and that includes the heart, arteries, and veins
Coaxing	persistent gentle persuasion
Combat	Fighting between armed forces
Commotion	a state of confused and noisy disturbance
Concubine	a woman who lives with a man but has lower status than his wife or wives, a mistress
Consummated	the completion of a thing
Contrive	To devise, plan, fabricate, create an undesirable situation
Coronation	the ceremony of crowning a sovereign
Creeper	any plant that grows along the ground, around another plant, or up a wall by means of extending stems or branches
Deciphered	to discover the meaning of something written badly or in a difficult or hidden way
Demolishing	to destroy or ruin, tear down
Demon/Demones	an evil spirit or devil
Deploy	to move, spread out, or place in position for some purpose
Derailing	obstruct (a process) by diverting it from its intended course
Destruct	serving or designed to destroy

Dignity	the state or quality of being worthy of honour or respect
Dwells	live in or at a specified place
Emperor	a sovereign ruler of an empire
Exile	the state of being barred from one's native country, typically for political or punitive reasons
Expiratory volume	measures how much air a person can exhale during a breath
Gamut	the complete range or scope of something
Grave situation	very serious, important, and worrying situation
Gravitate	move towards or be attracted to a person or thing
Guesstimate	a calculation of the size or amount of something when you do not know all the facts
Guru	GU - ignorance RU - remover - the remover of ignorance
Harsh	unpleasantly rough or jarring to the senses
Hissing	make a sharp sibilant sound as of the letter s
Incognito	in a way that conceals one's true identity
Indulged	allow (someone) to enjoy something desired
Inkling	a slight knowledge or suspicion; a hint
Inspiratory volume	measures how much air a person can inhale during a breath
Jowar crop	a variety of sorghum, Sorghum vulgare, extensively cultivated in Asia and Africa, used to make flatbreads
Lapse	an accidental or temporary decline or deviation from an expected or accepted condition or state; a temporary falling or slipping from a previous standard
Lashes out	hit or kick out at someone or something
Lava	hot liquid rock that comes out of the earth through a volcano
Manoeuvring	move skilfully or carefully
Mantra	"Manaha thrayathe ithi mantra" - that which helps us transcend the mind
Metaphor	a figure of speech in which a word or phrase is applied to an object or action to which it is not literally applicable
Meticulous	showing great attention to detail; very careful and precise
Nostrils	either of the two openings in the nose through which air moves when you breathe
Nun	a member of a female religious group whose members promise to obey the orders of the leader of the group, to be poor, and not to marry
Oblivious	not aware of or concerned about what is happening around one
Ogresses	a female human-eating giant, or a cruel or terrifying person
Parampara	A tradition. An uninterrupted row or series, order, succession, continuation, mediation, tradition
Pastures	land covered with grass and other low plants suitable for grazing animals, especially cattle or sheep
Peepal Tree	The peepal tree is considered the mythical 'Tree of Life' or 'World Tree' of the Indian subcontinent. The peepal tree, also called Ficus religiosa, belonging to the family Moraceae, is a variation of the fig tree known as the bodhi tree
Peripherals	of, relating to, involving, or forming a periphery or surface part
Perturbed	troubled in mind: feeling or showing agitation: bothered, upset

Plight	An unpleasant condition, especially a serious, sad, or difficult one
Portico	a covered entrance to a building
Potential	having or showing the capacity to develop into something in the future
Precincts	the area within the walls or perceived boundaries of a particular building or place
Profusely	in large amounts
Prominent	Important, famous
Radiance	an expression of great happiness, hope, or beauty
Ransacking	go through (a place) stealing things and causing damage
Ravage	the destructive effects of something
Recuperate	To recover from illness or exertion
Refined	developed or improved so as to be precise or subtle
Refrain	stop oneself from doing something
Rejuvenate	give new energy or vigour to; revitalize
Relish	to like or enjoy something
Remote corner	A remote area, house, or village is a long way from any towns or cities
Renowned	famous for something
Renunciate	a person who formally rejects or gives up something, especially a religious person who has renounced a secular way of life
Rescue	an act of saving or being saved from danger or difficulty
Retinue	a group of advisers, assistants, or others accompanying an important person
Reverberating	(of a loud noise) be repeated several times as an echo
Ruckus	A noisy fight or disturbance
Savage	Fierce, violent, uncontrolled
Scriptures	the sacred writings of a religion
Seldom	almost never
Sheer	a very fine
Shri Guru	Guru who takes us from book knowledge to practical experience
Sneak peek	an opportunity to have a quick look at something such as a film before it is officially available
Spontaneity	the quality of being natural rather than planned in advance
Stark contrast	very different from (something else)
Stroll	walk in a leisurely way
Stubborn	difficult to move, remove, or cure
Stunned	so shocked that one is temporarily unable to react
Tranquil	free from disturbance, calm
Traversing	to move or travel through an area
Truce	an agreement between enemies or opponents to stop fighting or arguing for a certain time
Underpinning	a set of ideas, motives, or devices which justify or form the basis for something
Vicinity	the area around a place or where the speaker/viewer is
Vested	fully and unconditionally guaranteed as a legal right, benefit, or privilege
Vocal cord	folds of throat tissues that are key in creating sounds through vocalization
Vulnerable	exposed to the possibility of being attacked or harmed, either physically or emotionally

Wander, wandering	move slowly away from a fixed point or place
Withering	acting or serving to cut down or destroy
Yuga	In Sanskrit, means "a yoke" (joining of two things), "generations", or "a period of time" such as an age

ABOUT THE AUTHOR

Gomathi Siva Sankaran is an Indian living in Denmark, exploring cultural diversity by building relationships across the globe.

A student of life, Gomathi relishes new learning experiences.

Founder and CEO, of a Denmark-based startup – the Guiding Light Art Company or the GLAC. This startup uses art and yoga as basic tools to engage people in the change mindset and create a positive social impact.

Gomathi is also a censor to various university examinations in Denmark.

Prior to this startup, Gomathi had a 17-year-journey within Manufacturing, Banking, Pharmaceutical, shared services and Energy companies in various finance and project management capacities.

An MBA from Copenhagen Business School, Denmark, CPA from New Hampshire State Board, USA, and Change Management Practitioner certified by APMG International.

Gomathi started her change journey via GLAC in 2017 with her first yoga sessions for women. The GLAC's Studio was created between the years 2019 & 2020 with the celebrate diversity series of artwork and art classes for children, which is now gaining momentum amongst the children and their parents. Both the art and yoga sessions are designed in a way to help individuals especially the younger generation cope with challenges such as stress, anxiety, and/or find their voice for self-expression. These art projects support and encourage international and local community integration.

The Change Mindset, the yogic way, is a concept developed in 2023 under the GLAC Sadhana wherein Gomathi together with Tobias Lasota, has created a series of tutorial videos. This is the book version of the visual content.

Visit: www.glac-sadhana.com/ for the Change Mindset Program – the Yogic Way Workshops and much more.

www.ingramcontent.com/pod-product-compliance
Lightning Source LLC
LaVergne TN
LVHW070942160826
845679LV00022B/1883

9798897246700